O Come!

O Come!

Reflections, Questions, and Prayers
for the Days of Advent

ROBERT BOAK SLOCUM

RESOURCE *Publications* • Eugene, Oregon

O COME!
Reflections, Questions, and Prayers for the Days of Advent

Resource Publications
An Imprint of Wipf and Stock Publishers
199 W. 8th Ave., Suite 3
Eugene, OR 97401

www.wipfandstock.com

PAPERBACK ISBN: 979-8-3852-1444-0
HARDCOVER ISBN: 979-8-3852-1445-7
EBOOK ISBN: 979-8-3852-1446-4

VERSION NUMBER 02/29/24

Acknowledgments

The prayers for Advent 4 Wednesday, Thursday, Friday, and Saturday are drawn from my devotional journal *Seeing & Believing, Reflections for Faith* (Wipf & Stock).

Advent 1 Sunday

"the day of the Lord will come like a thief" (2 Pet 3:10)

Surprise! God shows up, God with us, even when it seems impossible. But sometimes you need to have your eyes open to see what's happening. Wake up! Open up! We may discover God active in our lives from the beginning and inviting us always closer. Suddenly we may recognize God with us, closer to us than we are to ourselves.

?

How is God active in your life? How does God show up for you? Are you ready for surprise in this Advent?

+

Surprise me today, Lord. Help me find you today. Awaken hope. Show me new life.

Advent 1 Monday

> "My heart is steadfast, O God, my heart is steadfast. I will sing and make melody. Awake my soul! Awake, O harp and lyre! I will awake the dawn." (Ps 108:1–2)

Wake up! Jesus comes to us and invites our best response. Eyes open. Fully alive. Hearts open. Don't miss this. Don't sleep through it. Sing your best song. Don't be shy. It's a new day, a new morning. Wake up!

?

Where do you see God today? How do you respond? What will you give back? What will you create? How can you share what you have received?

+

Come to me now, Lord. I welcome you. I welcome this new day. I welcome all you offer.

Advent 1 Tuesday

> "In the morning, Lord, you hear my voice; early in the morning I make my appeal and watch for you." (Ps 5:3) (BCP)

"First light" comes before dawn, the first hint of light in the dark night sky. Advent comes to us as the very beginning of Jesus' approach, the first light to dispel the darkness. Dawn is wonderful to see. The darkness may seem endless but suddenly there's a quiver of light and new hope. A new day is dawning, a new light in our hearts, possibilities before us, our Lord comes to us this morning.

?

What do you discover in this new day? What is possible? What is the "first light" of your heart?

+

God of this new day and every day, bring me your light and I will see. I will open my eyes. I will know your love. I will find you near. I will discover something new.

Advent 1 Wednesday

"Ho, everyone who thirsts, come to the waters" (Isa 55:1)

Jesus comes to save us. He comes to bring what we need. He is water for the thirsty, food for the hungry, relief for the hurting, healing for the broken, guidance for the lost, love for us all. He's the answer to prayer. He's the prayer in our hearts. And he's coming closer. He invites us to drink the water that quenches our thirst. He invites us to be satisfied.

?

What do you need? What can you share? How do you know God present? When have you felt called?

+

Holy One, give us what we need today. Help us to receive with thanks, and share. Fill our hearts to overflow with love.

Advent 1 Thursday

"The people who walked in darkness have seen a great light; those who lived in a land of deep darkness—on them light has shined." (Isa 9:2)

These are dark days, the shortest days of the year in terms of sunlight. These are dark days, with no shortage of threats and worries in every news cycle and in our lives. We yearn for light. New light is entering our world. It's just beginning. Sometimes we must look for it. Sometimes we need to look hard. Sometimes we discover the light already in us, and we can share it.

?

When are your darkest times? How do you find the light of Christ? What do you see? How does God find you?

+

Dear Lord, bring light into every dark night. Lighten the heavy load that seems too much. Draw near in every broken moment. Help us know your glory.

Advent 1 Friday

> "The one who made the Pleiades and Orion, and turns deep darkness into the morning, and darkens the day into night, who calls for the waters of the sea, and pours them out on the surface of the earth, the Lord is his name." (Amos 5:8)

This is a new beginning, a time of creation. God makes new things in a new time, and God renews us. This is a time of creation. Do you see it? It's love writ large. The maker of heaven and earth makes us and renews us. God creates a new heart in us. God makes us a new people and invites us into creation. We can share his work of renewal in this place.

?

How do you see God in the world around us? Do you find God revealed in nature? How do you witness God's creation? Do you experience God's work of creation in your own life?

+

Blessed are you, Lord, God of creation, help us see your beauty surrounding us. Help us find you present in others, and in your wonderful creation. Help us to protect what we have received.

Advent 1 Saturday

> "A voice cries out: 'In the wilderness prepare the way of the Lord, make straight in the desert a highway for our God.'" (Isa 40:3)

God is coming to us in all kinds of times. Christ comes with love, hope, salvation—but never by force. Love invites welcome and a choice to accept love. God comes with power but never overpowers. In this season Christ comes to us new, as if for the first time. It's a new year, a new beginning. The Advent of God in our world. There's light in the darkness, warmth in the cold. God's invitation is for us, calling us to wake up, stand up, and be ready. Prepare the way of the Lord, make straight a highway that leads to our heart.

?

What are the paths that lead you to God? How do you find them? How do you recognize them? How do you travel them? Are there obstacles for you to remove on your path to God?

+

Holy God, help us to be ready to receive your love. Let us prepare the way to know you better and share what you give us. Help us open the doors of life.

Advent 2 Sunday

> "But, in accordance with his promise, we wait for new heavens and a new earth, where righteousness is at home." (2 Pet 3:13)

Christ is with us and comes to us for transformation of our world. Our Lord is no escape hatch or other-worldly diversion. We pray for God's kingdom to come on earth as in heaven. We pray for God's kingdom of justice, righteousness, and mercy. We celebrate God's gift. We pray for a place where people are treated fairly and included with love. God's love changes everything. God is coming for righteousness. This advent is for us; Christ comes for us.

?

How can we provide a home for God's righteousness? What can we do that makes a difference for others? How does God inspire us to share our gifts?

+

Holy God, you make all things new. Come to us and be near. Let us welcome your coming to us in love, your advent. Renew us and help us make a new start today.

Advent 2 Monday

"For God alone my soul in silence waits; from him comes my salvation." (Psalm 62:1) (BCP)

This is the hardest time of the year to slow down, to "take time," to wait. There are wonderful things for us to see in this new year, but we can miss them if we hurry. We need to make room for Christ's approach. The Lord may surprise us at an unexpected time. Our attentive listening reflects our love. We offer back our patience, and our willingness to wait. Nothing on our agenda is more important than this. We can listen.

?

What will God show us today? What will we hear? What do we discover when we wait? How has God surprised you?

+

Most patient God, help me to be still and wait quietly for you. Help me to make room for you in my life. Let me listen and receive your love. Let me clear space for you. Hear me now.

Advent 2 Tuesday

> "Get you up to a high mountain, O Zion, herald of good tidings; lift up your voice with strength, O Jerusalem, herald of good tidings, lift it up, do not fear; say to the cities of Judah, 'Here is your God!'" (Isa 40:9)

God comes to us with good news, and brings hope, comfort, and love. The Advent of Christ is the good news of God's approach to save us. The light of Christ casts out darkness and brings new clarity. The hope of Christ breaks through despair. Christ's presence invites us to an adventure of faith with possibilities beyond anything we can imagine. The love of Christ overcomes fear. Together in Christ we discover freedom to live the life of salvation and share it with others. We have good news to declare!

?

Does love overcome fear in your life? Have you known Christ present in difficult times? Does this Advent season bring new hope for you? What is your good news? How can you share it?

+

Loving God, show me your light and strengthen me with your love. Help me let go of worries and every distraction that would turn my eyes from you. Let me share the love that saves. Let me share the good news of your life.

Advent 2 Wednesday

> "Then I heard the voice of the Lord saying, 'Whom shall I send, and who will go for us?' And I said, 'Here am I send me!'" (Isa 6:8)

Jesus is born into the world for us and our salvation. Jesus comes in love because that's who God is. God loves us and shares divine life with us. God's love is free. We don't have to qualify or earn it. But we're called to receive God's love and share it. Praying, growing in faith, knowing God—changes us, makes us new. As we engage God's generosity we can grow in giving. As we receive God's forgiveness we can forgive others. As we know God's love we can love abundantly and share it. If we listen for Christ's approach with patience we may find ourselves called to action when the time is right. Our quiet in this season is rich soil and fertile for growth in faith.

?

Where does God send you today? What is God's surprise for you? How does God inspire you? Do you see a new direction? What new steps can you take?

+

My Lord and my God, help me to put my faith into action and share your love in the world. Strengthen me to move forward. Be present in every moment. Let me give generously. Send me in love.

Advent 2 Thursday

> "As the deer longs for the water-brooks, so longs my soul for you, O God. My soul is athirst for God, athirst for the living God; when shall I come to appear before the presence of God? (Ps 42:1–2)(BCP)

Eagerly we look for God's approach in our life. Without God we're dry, parched, empty. Our Lord comes to us in our darkness and confusion and we begin to see new light. Christ comes to us with healing love when we are in pain. Our Lord invites us to drink deep from the well of grace and know a love that delights us. God will not leave us thirsty. We yearn for this touch, God's appearing. Our Lord shows up in our lives constantly. We need to see what God reveals.

?

What does God show you today? How do you discover Christ's presence? How does God surprise you? How will you respond?

+

Dear God, I seek you. I yearn for you. Bring hope and grace to times that are dry. Bring light to times that are dark. Bring warmth to times that are cold. Bring completion to everything that is broken. Bring the life we need.

Advent 2 Friday

> "Every valley shall be lifted up, and every mountain and hill be made low; the uneven ground shall become level, and the rough places a plain. Then the glory of the Lord shall be revealed, and all people shall see it together, for the mouth of the Lord has spoken." (Isa 40:4–5)(NRSV)

Are you ready? Are you prepared for Christ coming to you? We don't have to make it happen. Grace is free. God will find us. But the barriers between us and God can obstruct. We can hinder our own salvation. Advent is a good time to remove the obstacles and stumbling blocks to faith. Preparing the way for Christ's approach may have little to do with changing the landscape or geography and everything to do with change in us. We can prepare our hearts. We can begin to remove whatever comes between us and God. We can claim time to slow down, listen, pray. We can hear God's call and discover new possibilities to share grace with others. We can reflect the light of Christ in a darkening world. The new landscape can be in us to welcome God's Advent.

?

How do you prepare for Christ's coming? Does anything obstruct God's approach for you? Do you need to make any changes? What do you hope for in this season? How will your landscape change?

+

Most generous Lord, help me push aside everything that comes between us, whatever gets in the way or keeps me apart from you. Draw us together.

Advent 2 Saturday

"Send out your light and your truth, that they may lead me, and bring me to your holy hill and to your dwelling." (Ps 43:3)(BCP)

Do you ever feel alone? Unsure of your direction? The light of Christ enters the world for guidance. Christ comes to us for love and our salvation. We are free to choose our path, but we are never abandoned by God. We are not left in the dark. Christ comes to bring us home. The light of Christ penetrates our darkness and whatever obscures hope. Christ is our pioneer, our leader, the one who goes before and shows us the way. We know him with each step.

?

Where do you find Christ in your life? Where does he lead you today? Does Christ offer you a new path? Where are you going?

+

In every step, Lord, be with me. Help me find the way; show me the path to you. Guide me to discover your love today.

Advent 3 Sunday

"And the one who was seated on the throne said, 'See, I am making all things new.'" (Rev 21:5)
"Sing to the Lord a new song, for he has done marvelous things." (Ps 98:1) (BCP)

We are made new in Christ. Our Lord comes to us as we are, but will not leave us as we were. The old wounds, the broken pieces of our lives, are bound up and made whole in Christ. God renews us to make a new start. This is a season of new beginnings, a clean slate prepared by our creator, a time to start fresh. A new day is breaking, and we may be surprised to see ourselves in its light. We're not alone. Love seeks us out and draws us together. Christ comes for love, saving us, inviting our response. We can offer ourselves. We can sing his praises, share his love, and include others. We can be made new.

?

How is God making your life new? How are the broken pieces of life made whole in Christ? How can you offer yourself? How will you sing God's praises (with or without music, with or without words)?

+

Gentle and loving God, help me find myself in the light of your love. Guide me to make a new life. Help me grow in faith. Let me find your love in me. Help me share it. Draw us all together in you.

Advent 3 Monday

"Put your trust in God; for I will yet give thanks to him, who is the help of my countenance, and my God." (Ps 43:6)(BCP)

Jesus comes to us in the midst of our darkness, mistrust, and confusion. It may be hard for us to trust if we've faced betrayal in the past. We may be reluctant to surrender control or put ourselves at risk to step forward in faith. Trust is at the heart of all we believe. We trust God's love and invitation for us. Like the fishermen who left their nets to follow Jesus (Mark 1:16–20), we may have no idea where we're going or what will happen in the future. But we trust our Lord will be with us on a surprising journey that saves. Knowing Jesus, trusting him, makes it possible for us to move past our old habits and distractions to follow our Lord. It's a new day.

?

What does trust in God mean for you? How do you live your trust in God? Is trust difficult for you? What helps? Where is God leading you today?

+

God of love, I don't know where I'm going but I know I'm not alone. You walk with me. Help me to find balance, foundation, and direction. Guide me home to you. Guide me on the way.

Advent 3 Tuesday

> "The people who walked in darkness have seen a great light; those who lived in a land of deep darkness—on them light has shined. You have multiplied the nation, you have increased its joy; they rejoice before you as with joy at the harvest, as people exult when dividing plunder. For the yoke of their burden and the bar across their shoulders, the rod of their oppressor, you have broken as on the day of Midian." (Isa 9:2–4)

Christ comes into our world to deliver us from sin and death, fear and hopelessness, isolation and hurt. The light we begin to see in Advent is our invitation to live, to heal, to come together. Our Lord delivers us from everything that separates us from loving God and each other; and from everything that separates us from ourselves. Christ delivers us from every diversion and distraction, every idol and deception that makes us less than we're called to be. This is God's grace, a gift of divine love, but also an invitation for our response. God sets us free to live but we must choose it. God offers us love without end but we must accept it. We may know God's love as we receive it, allowing love to shape us and helping us share love with others. That's our deliverance from every obstacle and hindrance to life that saves.

?

Do you struggle with obstacles to God's love that you would like to remove? How do you say *yes* to God? How will you share Christ's love? How does Christ's presence in your life make a difference for you? How do you see God's light?

＋

Holy God, let your love dawn with new light in my heart. Bring healing, hope, and inspiration. Help us to respond with love. Let us accept your wonderful gift.

Advent 3 Wednesday

> "As it is written in the prophet Isaiah, 'See, I am sending my messenger ahead of you, who will prepare your way; the voice of one crying out in the wilderness: 'Prepare the way of the Lord, make his paths straight.'" (Mark 1:2)

Have you heard a lonely voice? Have you been a lonely voice? Sometimes we may feel we're not being heard. Sometimes we forget to listen. We may find ourselves in a wilderness of confusion, doubt, and conflict. But we're not alone. We may see first light, the newly breaking day. We may begin to hear a call to prepare and make ready. We can let God in. We may be surprised by discovering Christ present with us in daily life. It helps if we're watching, listening. Prepare the way!

?

Has God found you when you felt alone? Have you been surprised by God? When has God found you in the wilderness? How can you prepare your heart?

+

Search me out, Lord, and know me. Find me in the dark and guide me to light. Stir up my energy, my generosity, my life. Let me prepare for your advent to me. Help me find my home in you.

Advent 3 Thursday

"I wait for the Lord; my soul waits for him; in his word is my hope. My soul waits for the Lord, more than watchmen for the morning, more than watchmen for the morning." (Ps 130:4–5)(BCP)

Waiting isn't easy. We're out of control. Things aren't happening on our schedule. There may be no end in sight. We must wait. Waiting for God means we focus on our Lord instead of ourselves. We pause our impatience and agenda. We may watch for some time without a glimpse of what we seek. It's worth the wait. The first signs of light can bring joy in the morning. We'll see more clearly as the new day comes. We can be patient to wait and eager to see. We may not be expecting what awaits us, the beauty of God.

?

What do you hope for? When have you waited for it? Were you impatient for it? Restless? How do you know it when it appears? How does it change you?

+

Gentle Lord, help me to be patient. Help me not to rush. Help me to relax when I am clutching my agenda, my plan, my timing—too tight! Guide my heart. Let me watch for your new day.

Advent 3 Friday

"How dear to me is your dwelling, O Lord of hosts! My soul has a desire and longing for the courts of the Lord; my heart and my flesh rejoice in the living God. The sparrow has found her a house and the swallow a nest where she may lay her young; by the side of your altars, O Lord of hosts, my King and my God." (Ps 84:1–2)(BCP)

Where do you belong? In our lives we may live in many houses; we may call many places our home. Like soldiers returning home from war, we may find ourselves homeward bound, seeking a place of rest that's our own. We seek our true home. Christ brings us home, and we find our true home with him and each other in his name. We long for that homeplace and want to share it. Advent comes with a challenge and an invitation to see our true home in Christ, surrounded by love. That's where we belong.

?

Where is your home in Christ? How do you find it? How do you know it? How can you share it? How does it feel to be home in Christ?

+

Gracious Lord, help me find my home with you. Guide me through wanderings and confusion to the place where I belong. Let me find you near when I feel alone. Open the door. I will stay.

Advent 3 Saturday

"For now we see through a glass, darkly; but then face to face." (1 Cor 13:12)(KJV)

We yearn for the completion of God's love in us. Today we can know Christ's presence in our lives, but not yet in fullness. As we come to know God, we want to see even more clearly. We want to know God without interruption, without obstacle, without distraction. We express this yearning, this longing for the fullness of God in Advent. It's a new beginning, the dawning of a new day, the beginning of a new life. It's so wonderful, and yet it's a beginning that makes us feel our need for completion even more sharply. We want to see God face to face and we cry out for more. We reach out in hope. *O come!*

?

How do you see Christ to be present with you today? What gets in the way? What needs to change for you to grow in relationship with God? Has God surprised you? What helps you to know God?

+

Open my eyes, Lord, and let me see you everywhere. Surprise me with your presence and love. Guide me on my next adventure. Amaze me with your generosity. Open my eyes to see you present with me.

Advent 4 Sunday

"See, the Lord God comes with might, and his arm rules for him; his reward is with him, and his recompense before him. He will feed his flock like a shepherd; he will gather the lambs in his arms, and carry them in his bosom, and gently lead the mother sheep." (Isa 40:10–11)

God comes in power; God comes in love. Christ's Advent changes everything for the sake of love. In love we see with new eyes. In love we find new capacity to give and receive. In love we welcome each new approach of Christ to be with us. We know God's love even more deeply as we share the gift with others. Our Lord gathers us together and gently leads us. God takes us beyond ourselves and our limitations.

?

How does God come to you? How have you been changed in love with Jesus? What have you given and received with God's help? How does God change your heart? What do you want to change in your life? What can be your first step to change?

+

O good Shepherd, find me when I seem to be lost. Search me out in my confusion. Guide me when I begin to struggle. Call me and I will come. Carry me gently home.

Advent 4 Monday

"Rejoice in the Lord always; again I will say, Rejoice. Let your gentleness be known to everyone. The Lord is near." (Phil 4:4–5)

Jesus comes to us for our great joy. Our Lord brings light, hope, peace, and salvation. He invites us to a life worth living. He invites us to rejoice. He beckons us to a dance of life that's filled with love. He calls us to share the abundance of his love instead of scarcity and fear. We know God's love more deeply as we love more generously. In Christ we have much to share, and it's a joy. God may be visible in the world when gifts of time and attention are shared in love. Eyes brighten and smiles appear as our Lord approaches and we see new light. We can celebrate. It's joy.

?

How do you know Christ present in your life? When do you rejoice? When have you shared your joy? How have you been generous? How do you celebrate God's love? What difference does God's presence make in your life?

+

Holy God, help me to make room for you in my life. Guide me to be quiet and listen. Let me celebrate each of your amazing gifts with joy, and share your abundance. Let me help others to rejoice in you.

Advent 4 Tuesday

"In the morning, Lord, you hear my voice; early in the morning I make my appeal and watch for you." (Ps 5:3) (BCP)

Jesus is our hope and expectation. We look for him in trust; he will find us. We wait in confidence for our savior; we seek him eagerly. We know his approach means everything for us. He comes to us just as we are but will not leave us as we were. It's the adventure of a lifetime. His love is our completion. He will not leave us without comfort. He will not leave us on our knees. He invites us to stand and move forward. He leads us into a surprising future. He guides us on new paths we can trust. We wait and watch eagerly for every clue. We are ready for every sign of God with us. We share the morning watch and wait for his first light.

?

Where is God leading you today? When has God surprised you? How do you discover Christ present in your life? When has our Lord found you? How does God's love make today a new day for you? What are your next steps? What does Christ's first light reveal to you?

+

Prepare my way to you, most loving God. Make my rough places smooth. Let my heart be ready. Prepare my heart for your coming. Bring light to my darkness; bring peace to my stress and fear. Guide my every step. Draw me closer to you.

Advent 4 Wednesday

"You know what time it is, how it is now the moment for you to wake from sleep. For salvation is nearer to us now than when we became believers; the night is far gone, the day is near." (Rom 13:11–12)

Wake up! Christ comes to us but we need to be awake to see him; we need to be alert to know him active in our lives. This is no time for distraction. Our Lord's coming to us is the start of a new season in life; Christ's advent is for our renewal. Christ invites us into a relationship of love that saves us. God invites a walk together that deepens our love with every step. The new day begins and darkness gives way to light. Christ's love touches our hearts and spreads. In Christ we open our eyes; we live, discover, and share the gifts we have received. The sun rises on a new day.

?

How have you grown in faith? Has your relationship with God changed over time? What helps you to draw closer to God? How do you find God active in your life? Have you felt surprised by God's presence in your life?

+

Show your love today, Lord. Help us to see you near and find you everywhere. Let us soar in your sky. Touch our hearts. Show your bright glory. Lead us into brilliant light.

Advent 4 Thursday

> "Listen! I am standing at the door, knocking; if you hear my voice and open the door, I will come in to you and eat with you, and you with me." (Rev 3:20)

God invites us to love, calling us to a life that transforms us. But this gift can't be forced. We are no lovers unless we choose the gift; and it's no lover who forces the gift on another. But God our lover doesn't give up on us or walk away. Even if we're distracted or slow to respond, Christ keeps knocking at the door. This love endures. God invites and God persists. In this Advent and every day, God approaches and invites us to share new life that saves. *Listen*!

?

When have you heard Christ knocking on your door? How did you respond? Did God keep inviting if you kept your distance? If you said yes to God, what did you discover? What has changed?

+

Dear Lord, help us listen for you. Be present. Always remind us you are near, standing at the door, knocking to enter our lives. Open our eyes so we may see; open our hearts so we may love. Open our hands so we may serve and give generously. Come now, come today, come in this Advent.

Advent 4 Friday

> "And I heard a loud voice from the throne saying, 'See, the home of God is among mortals. He will dwell with them; they will be his peoples, and God himself will be with them; he will wipe every tear from their eyes. Death will be no more; mourning and crying and pain will be no more, for the first things have passed away." (Rev 21:3–4)

Christ comes to bring us together. His love displaces isolation and division as we respond and gather in his name. Light scatters the darkness. God includes us all, calling us out of separation from each other and God. In the light of Christ's Advent, we see. The divine love drawing us together is stronger than anything that would tear us apart. Sharing God's love can help to make smooth the roughness between us. We can seek to understand the other and find common ground. We can appreciate perspectives different from our own. We may be surprised to discover how much we have in common. We can take the possible steps to reconcile when there has been disagreement. We can seek to let go of grudges and old hurts. We can forgive and accept forgiveness, and forgive ourselves. We know we are forgiven and enfolded in God's love, drawn together by grace. We are one body in Christ, united in him.

?

How do you know Christ with and through others? How does your faith help you reach out to others and know them? Have you found God in others and in your relationships with them? How does God help us to come together? What steps can you take to heal division, estrangement, separation?

+

Draw nearer Lord, you bring new courage. Help us to welcome your approach, especially in this Advent season. Help us to be ready. Strengthen us to take steps of healing and reconciliation. Give us grace to let go of old hurts. Help us to forgive others and ourselves; let others forgive us. Guide us through all our doubts and worries. Bring the light of your love. Heal our divisions and help us to draw together with others in the one body of your love. Let us share your peace.

Advent 4 Saturday

> "Now there was a great wind, so strong that it was split-ting mountains and breaking rocks in pieces before the Lord, but the Lord was not in the wind; and after the wind an earthquake, but the Lord was not in the earth-quake; and after the earthquake a fire, but the Lord was not in the fire; and after the fire a sound of sheer silence."
> (I Kgs 19:11b-12)

Christ comes to us constantly, and sometimes in unexpected ways and times and seasons. God's appearance may not be dramatic. Christ's presence may take us by surprise. We may find Christ present in silence or sound. We may be alone or with others, in joyful times or great stress. God's love may overwhelm us, or it may seem like a hint or a whisper. It helps if we keep listening. God will amaze us with love!

?

When have you found Christ present in your life and world? How does Advent help you listen for God? How does listening change your life? What do you discover about God and yourself in this season? What do you see differently because of Christ's coming to you?

+

Touch all our hearts with your devotion. Open our eyes so we may see. And in our darkness bring salvation. Until our life is one with thee.

+

O come, Emmanuel! Be with us! *O come!*

www.ingramcontent.com/pod-product-compliance
Lightning Source LLC
Chambersburg PA
CBHW060646030426
42337CB00018B/3469